spot

BABY ANIMALS

BABY BEARS

by K.C. Kelley

AMICUS

bamboo

claws

Look for these words and pictures as you read.

nose

tongue

What's splashing in the water?
It's a baby bear!

There are many kinds of bears.
They have babies called cubs.

See the cub's claw?
They have five claws on each foot.
Bears use claws to hold food.

See its nose?

Polar bear cubs have black noses.

They can smell well.

nose

tongue

See the cub's tongue?
Sun bear cubs have long tongues.
They lick honey from a bee's nest.

See that bamboo?
Panda cubs live in China.
They eat bamboo. Crunch!

bamboo

This baby brown bear
finds its mother.
It's time for a snack!

bamboo

claws

Did you find?

nose

tongue

Amicus Readers and Amicus Ink are imprints of Amicus
P.O. Box 1329, Mankato, MN 56002
www.amicuspublishing.us

Library of Congress Cataloging-in-Publication Data

Names: Kelley, K. C., author.
Title: Baby bears / by K.C. Kelley.
Description: Mankato, MN : Amicus, [2018] | Series: Spot. Baby animals | "Spot is an imprint of Amicus."
Identifiers: LCCN 2017022654 (print) | LCCN 2017034978 (ebook) | ISBN 9781681513300 (pdf) | ISBN 9781681513164 (library binding : alk. paper) | ISBN 9781681522500 (pbk. : alk. paper)
Subjects: LCSH: Bear cubs--Juvenile literature. | Readers (Primary) | Vocabulary.
Classification: LCC QL737.C27 (ebook) | LCC QL737.C27 K45 2018 (print) | DDC 599.78--dc23
LC record available at https://lccn.loc.gov/2017022654

Printed in China

HC 10 9 8 7 6 5 4 3 2 1
PB 10 9 8 7 6 5 4 3 2 1

Megan Peterson, editor
Deb Miner, series designer
Patty Kelley, book designer
Producer/Photo Research:
Shoreline Publishing Group LLC

Photos:
Cover: Holly Kuchera/Dreamstime.com.
Inside: Dreamstime.com: Holly Kuchera 1, JLHope 2tl, Carmen Craig 2tr, Donyanedomam 2bl, Kaye Eileen Oberstar 2br, Kslynskyy 3, Farinoza 4, Isselee 5, Rinus Baak 6, Andreanita 8, Peter Masek 10, David Hoffman Photography 14. Minden Pictures: Katherine Feng 12.